Minimalism

The Advice On Minimalism For Simple Living At Home
Includes A Guide To Becoming Minimalist, As Well As
Recommendations For Designing Beauty, Balance, And A
Sustainable Lifestyle In Order To Save Money And
Reduce Stress; Tiny Spaces, And Net Zero Living

Vladimir Feldmann

TABLE OF CONTNET

Clothes/Accessory 1

Taking Care Of Your Clutter 4

Clear All Of Your Flat Surfaces. 19

Intentionality Is Minimalism. 35

The Reasons To Try Minimalism 62

Why Embrace Minimalism 72

Give Away, Sell, Donate, And Discard. 85

How Living Minimally Lowers Stress 103

Substance Minimalism Is International. 118

Minimise: Decluttering And Reducing. 139

Clothes/Accessory

The wardrobe, or any area of a room used to store clothes, is another important area to focus on. Many might argue that a storeroom simply isn't big enough, and although that argument may hold up in many cases, there's also the argument that we're trying to fit too much stuff into the closet. One way to help fit everything inside might be to give the storage area a facelift.

Examine everything that is in your storage area. Decide on a time frame and state that you will say goodbye to an item if it hasn't been worn in "x" months. Naturally, depending on your surroundings, this won't affect rare items but try to pull off as few of these things as possible. Select a variety of socks, jeans, shirts, and other items you feel comfortable wearing, and store them in your storage area. Continue to manage this item quantity and keep your storage area organized. Managing your personal affairs might be a wonderful idea, offering you a fresh start and a new appearance. Keep colors that look amazing on you to add to your modest wardrobe. Maintaining colors that are starkly different from one another works wonderfully because they go with almost anything.

There may be different things you can store depending on the size of your storeroom. Carefully consider those items, determining once more whether they are necessary or valuable enough to take up your valuable space. Anything you don't think is worthwhile or enjoyable should be moved to a different room in the house or out of the house entirely.

In brief:

You could get away with using a moderate room only for necessities. Because there is so much outside those four walls, minimalism encourages people to go beyond space and onto other things in daily life. Keeping the space basic creates an amazing atmosphere for a peaceful night's sleep and facilitates getting ready and venturing outside.

Reducing Space in Garages, Attics, Basements, and Other Storage Areas

This section will deal with storing items in areas where we typically store items and then forget about them. These spaces include our storm cellars, lofts, carports, or any similar area used for storage. Even while these spaces are fantastic for storing larger or infrequent items, we frequently conceal items we want to handle later—but that later never materialize.

Taking Care Of Your Clutter

If you decide to declutter an area of your life, try to stick with it until you're done. You don't have to turn this into a crusade; you may take your time. To incorporate these areas into your life, you can work on them one time as follows:

- Specific rooms within the house
- The wardrobe
- The kitchen cabinets
- The refrigerator and freezer
- The furniture
- The kid's toys—involve them
- The bathroom cabinets
- The paperwork—go paperless!

Keeping a minimalist journal helps you to schedule specific times to do tasks. There's a reason I informed you about mindfulness. When you start a task, turn off all outside distractions and work on it for at least 45 minutes, pausing for ten minutes before continuing. You will do the activity more quickly if you focus on it and don't allow your mind to stray into other ideas or periods.

When it comes to clothing, arrange everything on the bed and proceed with each item individually. It goes if it doesn't improve the way you feel and look! You have complete control over how this is arranged, although some dress agencies will take your clothes and pay you for them after they are sold. Additionally, homeless shelters are constantly in need of warm clothing. It may surprise you that old woollies are a great resource for dog shelters looking to provide a warm, comfortable home for a pet while its owner is away. It doesn't squander anything. It's just the redistribution of things that don't improve your life.

To persuade you, I would like you to close the door from the outside while you are standing outside the main room where you and your family gather. Now open it, but first notice what draws your attention. This is meant to be the center of your existence. Many people notice that objects they would rather not see as focus points, such as stacks of paper, books scattered about, and DVDs removed from their boxes, catch their attention. The main attraction in a minimalized home should always be something you enjoy looking at, like the painting hidden behind all the junk you've accumulated over the past 20 years!

Additionally, keep in mind that less is always more. Individuals cram their homes with collections, which they occasionally outgrow but dust and polish them every week without fail. Consider the newly available space. Imagine how amazing one item could appear in its place. You have the last say over what should remain and what should go, but many small collections require labor on your part, so you must determine if they are worthwhile.

The physical items you discard from a room can be put in the garage in the proper bags so you can dispose of them as soon as possible—either by giving them away, throwing them in the trash, or selling them at a garage sale or shop. It's impossible to overstate the liberation and freedom of clearing out a single room. It is, therefore, advisable to work in one room at a time. Remove the floral curtains that are too busy to go with the patterned flooring. It's all about keeping things simple, which enlarges the space and lets in more light because the draperies were blocking the light's natural path. You are restoring your home to what you require to survive. The house was vacant when you purchased it. You made the decisions about what went there, but as your life changed, so too should the way you show your house to guests and yourself.

There are numerous strategies for reducing housework. On your dressing table, how many makeup bottles are there? By clearing out the top drawer and purchasing a makeup tray, you can keep all of these items in one location and out of the way of dust, improving the room's appearance and requiring less maintenance. In my home, we have a very effective rule that the kids carry with them when they move out. You always leave a room more orderly than when you found it. My kids were trying to fix the oddly crooked painting in a tidy and minimalized house because there wasn't much else for them to do. Still, it also made the house incredibly livable, ready for unexpected guests, and enjoyable.

It's incredible how liberating it feels to let go of things. It won't take long to want to work on the next room and the next until you are free of everything that clogs your life and makes it hard if you go at your own pace, make the decisions, and finish one room. I kept before and after pictures in my minimalism journal, which reminded me of why I was doing what I was doing. The diary will help you stay on course if you start to feel like giving up. It will also assist your family to realize why the process is taking place and value the freedom it offers you both!

Chapter 2: The Positive Impact of Minimalism on Your Life

The primary benefit of moderation and maintaining a simpler lifestyle freed from the tight grasp of possessions is not a tranquil way of living. Cleaning your home involves more than just bumping your toe while you're trying to urinate at three in the morning, though that is a huge benefit.

One benefit of having fewer goods is that it entails having fewer obligations, which suggests greater freedom from the rat race. After you pay off that Mastercard, cancel it completely. We're not suggesting you give up on your school loans and put everything up for auction, but the topic of discussion is whether you need that fancy new coat you were about to charge to your Visa a few seconds ago. Yes, your monthly installment on your Visa maybe $15, but when you include in premium and charge card fees, that $100 coat quickly becomes a $150.00 coat—all at the expense of not making the whole payment upfront.

Could you have completed the task if you had just been given the option to pay with cash upfront? Even if this is accurate, why are you utilizing the Visa in the first place? If not, you will save $100.00, but you will also avoid paying the additional $50.00 in premiums and fees.

Fewer material belongings lead to greater freedom from the grind of pursuing your life's ambitions, like traveling to Ireland or kayaking in Yellowstone.

You may save that money to purchase a house of your own. No one tells you that owning a home is financially worthless.

Additionally, you can help the climate by leading a balanced lifestyle. You will have less to replace or discard if you own fewer items. Devaluing the items we own and the "essential stuff" we use can help reduce our impact on the climate and keep the earth we live on functional. The idea of constant commercialization is destroying the environment around us. Reduced item utilization suggests that fewer resources are fundamentally utilized to create the mounting materials and that the ecology is exposed to less pollution.

This balanced lifestyle also gives you more time to be productive. Less distractions from things around you should allow you to take the necessary time and care, which should then be focused on things that matter. Whether spending time with close ones or going for a walk in your favorite place to complete that crucial task in an area that makes you smile, freeing your life from numerous consumerist disruptions can enhance your level of satisfaction because it exchanges one source of care for another. You can fit so many more activities into that extra time that will improve the life you lead right now. For example, stress-relieving hobbies like yoga, meditation, exercise, gardening, hiking, fishing, and hunting are all things that many people just "do not have time for."

By giving away and getting rid of items you finally no longer need, you can relieve yourself of the relative abundance of disruptions. You can also dedicate a short period to these kinds of activities, which can also help you feel less stressed.

Not only that, but you can be sure that you are truly serving as an example for others. If you are a parent, your children will observe your behavior and learn how to conduct their lives like you do. Even if you detest how you spend so much money when you buy, your kids will see you do it and pick up that habit in later life, where they will struggle with similar issues.

If you can resolve those conflicts and live a more peaceful life, you will demonstrate to your children that this is how life is meant to be lived.

The same effect may impact friends, coworkers, and family members like your parents. In this section of the book, the phrase "be the change you wish to find on the planet" is quite apparent since it refers to the idea that the best method to affect change in those around you is to model that change for them. Instead of talking about it, making jokes about it, and telling other people it'ssmart, just do it yourself. Allow the change to enter your life and serve as concrete proof that others must make the same changes in their lives.

Obi-Wan Knowledge: Lessons from Exceptionally Well-Ordered Individuals

We've seen ways to arrange nearly all of your life's pillars. But I've also discovered that many people find it nearly impossible to live a life of organization (being a skilled organizer). Here are some wise recommendations to make the process easier and something you can do every day for a year, two years, or even forever.

Put everything in writing.

Write everything down and consult it whenever necessary, rather than depending solely on your memory. In a culture where technology is advanced, carrying a notebook everywhere is not necessary. Employ the resources available to you. These days, a smartphone is more than just a tool for communication. You may capture audio and take notes with apps like Evernote. It's the ideal location for idea storage. This is very useful because anything that is not in use gets stored deeper in our thoughts, comparable to computer RAMS. Putting everything down on paper gives your mind more time to do what it does best: create. It also significantly increases your productivity.

Clear All Of Your Flat Surfaces.

Ensure that every flat surface in your home, including your kitchen counter and work desk, is clutter-free. Clutter and flat surfaces draw each other in. I promise that if you set one object down on your flat surface and leave it there, it will draw in additional items. Keep only things intended for the countertops, and treat all your flat tops as no-dumping zones.

Maintain everything's proper position.

This is the significant one. The fact that we don't set apart spaces for each of our necessities is one of the main reasons why most of us struggle to stay organized for extended periods. Create a specific area for everything you might need to store in the "junk drawer" rather than encouraging a "junk drawer" mentality (be sure to adhere to the advice we previously looked at). Ensure every item has a designated space, especially those you use frequently. Consider the things you cherish as "little people"; they, too, require a place to live. An object immediately turns into clutter and becomes a barrier to your mental clarity if it becomes homeless. By designating certain locations, you can be sure that you won't have to browse a variety of "other" objects to get what you need. You avoid a migraine and save time by doing this.

Keep yourself busy.

To be frank with one another, I would admit that decluttering and organizing is an ongoing effort. There will always be that one item that doesn't belong there, even if your house or area has attained organizational Zen and has a great atmosphere. Bees are constantly engaged in transporting something to another location. Take up this mindset. Whenever you are in a room, try to locate anything that isn't in its proper place and move it there. This is especially helpful for simple products, including socks, toys, and coffee mugs.

Put it in the file.

Most individuals tend to pile things up to do them later. The only issue is that if you develop this habit, you will constantly find an excuse to put off organizing a pile of stuff, even though that does not exactly prevent catastrophe. In contrast, file one thing. Make a command center or "inbox" for all incomings if you receive a lot of invoices, pamphlets, and periodicals. You can modify this approach to fit every aspect of your life.

Regularly declutter

You will never get the complete rewards of living a life without clutter if you wait to declutter until your drawers overflow. Whatever the size of your space—whether ample or insufficient—try to declutter as frequently as you can. The perfect time to declutter is not set in stone. By all means, declutter once weekly if you feel comfortable doing so only once. A month is fine if you feel comfortable doing it only once a month. Ensuring that there is not an excessive amount of time between periods is the key to constant decluttering. This is because you will become demotivated if you let the clutter get out of control.

What is minimalism defined as in Chapter 1?

A minimalistic pattern or style uses the fewest basic items possible to achieve the desired result.

However, in recent times, it has come to represent a manner of living that seeks to remove clutter from all facets of one's existence.

The main idea behind minimalism is to purge everything that doesn't add value or meaning to your life and just maintain what matters. It all comes down to trimming the surplus and concentrating your energy on what's left. We all have limited energy, opportunities, and space in our life. To make the most out of the circumstances, we must be mindful of how we spend each day.

We live in a world of distractions, so making time and space to savor life's pleasures can be challenging.

Our excessive concern with being overwhelmed by material, digital, and emotional waste results in increased anxiety and dissatisfaction.

The answer to this excess is minimalism.

A minimalist lifestyle is much more than just that, albeit that is its general outline. We typically associate it with power, status, safety, and pleasure. But the more you look outside of yourself for what you need, the more you have to give up, and the farther you get from yourself.

Minimalism pushes you to think little rather than hoping that thinking bigger will make the suffering disappear.

Minimalism aims to help you succeed more quickly by helping you prioritize the important things in life. There are numerous approaches to minimalism.

The purposeful preservation of the things that bring you joy while getting rid of the things that don't are known as minimalism.

Curating our belongings to best reflect our vision and ideals for our life is a notion that is known by many names, including simple living, modest living, purposeful living, and more.

It shouldn't overwhelm someone to consider minimalism. Minimalism can benefit you whether you live in an opulent home, a little cottage, or an apartment in the suburbs. You can use minimalism as a foundational principle and modify it to suit your requirements.

Is it feasible to have a minimalistic existence in only one area?

I recently finished reading a nice book titled "No Baggage" that described the adventures of two young people who traveled purposefully without any luggage, to the surprise of many. Reading the book made it obvious that neither of them was a minimalist in the traditional sense. Still, they had made decisions about their journey, qualifying it as "minimalist" travel. You are not truly a minimalist if you merely adhere to one or two principles of simplicity. That being said, there are elements of the minimalist concept that apply to every person's life and would be useful, such as keeping your home tidy, eating sensibly, managing your money, and letting go of material belongings.

How many individuals adhere to minimalism?

Though it is hard to estimate the number of minimalists in the USA, let alone the rest of the globe, there is undoubtedly a growing interest in simplicity. Millions of results will appear in your Google search if you enter any of the chapter's subtitles. There have been suggestions that Japan, whose culture is rooted in Zen Buddhism, could serve as a global model for minimalism. With over 100 million people living in Japan, it is safe to assume that millions of minimalists live worldwide.

Why is minimalism becoming more and more popular?

A response to a culture of materialism is minimalism. The 1980s saw increased consumption until the 2000 and 2008 stock market crashes. Since then, people have had to reconsider their priorities and methods of survival all around the world. We are residing in an era of remarkable change. But if we are to avert an ecological catastrophe, the consumerist manner of doing things cannot last. Minimalism provides a means for people to lead happy, sustainable lifestyles.

Consumerism and Minimalism

Consumerism pushes consumers to purchase items that are deemed "cool." The advertising industry aims to arouse people's desires and give them the impression that they are being deceived if they do not own the advertised goods. A family could easily survive on one person's earnings in the past, but that is no longer the case thanks to consumerism. Today, a family's total earnings may not be sufficient to meet all the requirements that are thought to be necessary for happiness. People who live in a society based on consumerism are compelled to get more and more. They have to incur debt if needed to get what they desire. The exact opposite is true with minimalism. It suggests that focusing on what is genuine, minimizing possessions, and practicing gratitude for what one already has can all lead to pleasure. It implies that acquiring fewer material possessions increases happiness.

We shall examine this conflict in greater detail in the upcoming chapter.

Before purchasing, inquire.

The next time you find yourself in a situation where you need to make a permanent purchase for your home or place of employment, ask yourself if it will enable you to maintain a minimalist lifestyle and maximize your capacity to live according to your true values. Don't buy it if the response is "no". By doing this, you may rewire your purchasing patterns and prevent fresh clutter from quickly reentering your life.

Adhere to Your Content

Always respect other people's ownership rights over items in your home if you cohabitate with others. You are free to purge your personal belongings but not those of others. I mean, you wouldn't want people to just toss away your belongings without asking? Yes, exactly!

Asking the people you live with first if they still need or desire the items you're thinking of getting rid of—and, more significantly, if it's okay with them—will show you respect for them. Suppose you dispose of their belongings without their consent. In that case, you'll only exacerbate the situation by encouraging them to accumulate more items in the fear that you might take them away at any time.

How Often Will You Use It?

Lastly, consider the question, "Will I need to use this anytime soon and on a regular basis?" when you go through each of your material belongings. If not, it ought to be a top choice for disposal. Recall that you should only hold onto items that will provide value to your life; these items may be useful or functional.

Intentionality Is Minimalism.

It is distinguished by its purpose, purity, and clarity. In essence, minimalism is purposefully highlighting the things we value most and eliminating anything that detracts from those things. It's a life that demands authenticity. It consequently forces improvements in nearly every aspect of your life.

FREEDOM FROM THE PASSION TO POSSESS IS MINIMALISM.

The belief in modern culture is that the good life is found in acquiring possessions—in poising as much as possible. They firmly feel that more is preferable and have unintentionally subscribed to the notion that happiness can only be obtained at a department store.

However, they are mistaken. Minimalism frees people from the all-consuming pursuit of perfection. It dares to seek happiness anywhere and gets off the consumption treadmill. Relationships, experiences, and self-care are highly valued. And it finds life in the process.

BEING FREE FROM MODERN MANIA IS MINIMALISM.

The world exists on a finite scale. We feel rushed, rushed, and overly exhausted. We put in long, intense hours at work to pay the expenses, but our debt just grows. We hop from one task to another, sometimes even multitasking in the process, but we never manage to finish anything. We maintain constant communication with others via our cell phones.

It discovers a way to detach. It aims to preserve only the essentials. It aims to retain the significance and eliminate the frivolous. And in doing so, it gives importance to the spontaneous pursuits that enrich life.

Chapter 2: Cutting Down on Your Connections

Everybody has people in their lives. There's no avoiding it, but do you have valuable people in your life? What about the friendships that drain your time and energy without providing anything in return? Imagine your most unwanted visitor in this situation, then picture yourself in a room with twenty of them! You would be so stressed out by the thought that you would not even consider it. But you let regular people drain your energies, and they do. In relationships, it is undoubtedly true that little is more. You must take the following action to maintain your sanity and truly enjoy your life rather than dread waking up every day.

Step 2 is to cut back on your friendships. After you've enumerated everyone, you should assess which friendships are good or bad. The negative kinds are as follows:

People who abuse you continuously and never return the favor

People who encroach on your personal space and whom you would rather avoid

People you hate phoning, yet you still do it

Individuals who utilize you as an emotional vent for their problems

Experts without experience

Among the positive kinds are the following:

People who reciprocate the same amount of favors

Individuals who motivate you

Individuals that elicit laughter

Individuals who can pay attention and provide candid criticism

Individuals who are fully aware of give-and-take

Positively influencing relatives

Since you cannot do much to get rid of relatives, I added them. Whether you like them or not, your relatives are still a part of your life. However, you can reduce your time with those relatives by making yourself less accessible. These detrimental factors in your life prevent you from developing. They hold you back, and if you give in to their manipulation, it won't help you at all since they will just keep abusing you. People who cause you pain are also negative, and you will be able to identify them by your sense of sensitivity. Positive people should replace negative ones since they are like sponges and will drain you of all your vitality and zest for life. But how exactly do you do that?

Saying "no" is among the first things you should learn as, if you always say "yes," you are not doing yourself any favors. Even while you might think of yourself as giving and appreciating the compliments you receive, when it comes to people like this, the praise is only given because they know you are willing to be a doormat. That is in no way genuine praise. The words they use are not worth it. Decide which friendships would make your life richer without them after you've made your list.

Many people in your lifetime will come and go, and while it may seem insensitive to ignore them, it's the only way you can move on constructively. Get yourself occupied with other activities.

Don't be there every time they call. Refrain from serving as a dumping ground for people who wish to undermine you. It is not selfish to do this; you must begin loving yourself. You'll understand what I mean when you picture this next scenario.

Layla surrounded herself with people and gained significance from the comments others made about her. Although she didn't have a high sense of self-worth, her negative and poisonous companions were draining her energy. She fell into a vicious cycle where she always followed everyone else's instructions out of fear of rejection. She lost any sense of self-respect and began to judge herself by the opinions of others, even though her actions consistently diminished the perception that people had of her. All she needed to do was alter her friendships and manage her time more effectively so that she could recognize her worth, but instead, she ended up taking antidepressants and seeing her doctor frequently. She didn't need more, just less.

After speaking with a psychotherapist for a while, Layla came to see that she had chosen the life she led. She gradually strengthened herself by volunteering on Saturdays and viewing herself as the kind and considerate person she truly was. We tend to overlook the obvious. We can like who we are; when we don't like who we are, we also don't draw in the correct individuals. We expose ourselves to the kind of mistreatment that Layla had committed against herself. You attract individuals who will like you for the same reasons that you do if you truly like who you are. For instance, someone who constantly seeks acceptance due to their insecurity will only attract those who take advantage of other people. They provide all of the input that someone requests but at a cost. In a similar vein, most individuals who enter violent relationships don't think highly of themselves. They believe that they have no rights outside of the abusive relationship, which is absurd. Everyone has the right to happiness and love. But, because of their self-hatred, they draw those looking for easily manipulated companions or partners.

Chapter 1: Greetings from Minimalism

Well done on your initial step towards minimalism. Hopefully, this lifestyle approach will give you the peace of mind you seek. You will learn about the foundations of minimalism in this chapter.

Minimalist Living: What Is It?

This is a manner of living where you get rid of everything you don't need or use anymore, leaving you with a minimalist home with the necessities. It also includes developing an attitude emphasizing simplicity and doing one task at a time with all your might.

The Advantages of Being Simple

Living a minimalistic lifestyle is a great approach to de-stress both outside and internally. It also aids in debt relief and financial savings. You also develop greater creativity and organization in your living and working environments. It also frees up a lot of your time because it requires less cleaning and upkeep of your surroundings. Above all, it's a sustainable way of living that you can easily maintain for however long.

Not at all dull

The minimalist lifestyle isn't inherently dull or uncreative, despite popular belief. It will only get monotonous if you allow it to. Ultimately, living a minimalist lifestyle just means getting rid of everything but the things that truly matter most to you. It is not dull if you value poetry, art, music, or travel above all else. Because your feeling of purpose is so much higher than the daily grind, you will even feel true happiness.

A Minimalist's Day in the Life

While every individual is unique and follows a different minimalist lifestyle, it wouldn't hurt to get a glimpse of a normal minimalist's day in and day out.

A minimalist is typically guided by a list of five or fewer essential tasks to complete each day. The minimalist completes one task at a time rather than jumping from one task to another or multitasking. The minimalist appreciates having a routine that allows them to complete each activity without feeling rushed and ensures they have time to unwind or engage in their favorite activities at the end of the day. Some minimalists prioritize their to-do list by placing chores connected to their passion first.

How to Adopt a Minimalist Way of Life

Once you decide to live a minimalist lifestyle, you can progressively purge everything superfluous from your life and narrow your attention to what truly counts. When you practice minimalism, you should bid farewell to debt, clutter, overworking yourself, procrastination, and emotional strain. You won't be able to embrace your values, passion, and purpose unless you accomplish this.

Living a simple lifestyle has no fixed guidelines. You don't need to stress over whether it's better to give up your automobile and large house or become a vegan. It matters that you live a much simpler life with greater physical, emotional, mental, and spiritual well-being.

Chapter 4: How Your Home Can Be Decluttered

Decluttering their home is often the first step towards leading a more minimalist lifestyle. Some people only take this one step, but we urge you to always adopt a declutteringmindset. Many people are unaware of the tension of possessing too many possessions. Disorganized and extra objects in our lives can lead to pressures that give us the impression that we ultimately do not have control, whether you are the type of person who continuously stubbles your pinky toe against the leg of that chair or who gets stressed out by all the books and papers in your office.

However, you are in charge.

Although it may seem easy enough, clearing up clutter in your home may rapidly become difficult for everyone who tries it. Whether an inanimate object represents a positive or negative aspect of our past, humans tend to attach emotional sentiment to it. This tendency alone can keep us from taking the necessary actions to free ourselves from the clutter that exists in our closets, let alone the clutter that takes up entire rooms.

Your first step should be making sure you know the difference between preserving memories and emotions. Positive memories are stored in photo albums, picture frames, and souvenirs. These objects bring back memories of times and people in our past. Eliminating these photos and priceless memories does not constitute decluttering a house. But your child's first crib and their homecoming costume are not the same thing.

The first is the size itself. The distinction between emotional and memory attachment is the other, though.

Looking at an object, such as a picture or the first garment your child wore home, can evoke memories of a specific physical place, person, and moment. This phenomenon is known as memory attachment. When you gaze at an item, such as a couch, cot, or antiquated piece of memorabilia, you are reminded of the feeling that once surrounded it, known as an emotional attachment. You can still clearly recall the first time you placed your child in their cot. You recall those tearful mornings when you had to wake up at all hours of the night to tend to your ailing child. You recall when they eventually outgrew their cot.

One is associated with a specific moment, whereas the other is associated with numerous moments that elicit strong emotional reactions.

Since it will initially be difficult to tell the two apart, some people arrange objects by size. But this is your distinction: an object you keep tends to be associated with a single event. In contrast, an item you give away evokes memories of several other occasions.

Do not panic; it will arrive in due course.

Getting assistance from someone is the best advice you can give to tidy your home. When it comes to holding that leather jacket you bought two years ago for an excursion you never went on; they will offer an unbiased evaluation. The tag is still on it. They will help you focus on your final objective while recognizing when giving anything away can be excessive.

Another thing to know is that, for many individuals, decluttering a home happens in phases rather than all at once.

It's difficult to let go of these emotional ties, one of the numerous reasons our "things" cause us so much stress. Surrounding ourselves with objects consistently eliciting emotions is taxing on our limbic systems, adrenal glands, and neural connections. For most people, feeling emotionally exhausted is just part of who they are, and they are often unaware of it!

Thus, begin in a single room. Make it your mission to declutter any space in your house by the end of the day. To raise money for other, more important things (like those pesky bills we all have to pay), bring in boxes and donate materials, or even organize a huge yard sale.

How To Invest In Books, Accessories, And Clothes Minimally

Adjusting your wardrobe and clothing is the first step towards living a simpler life. They store your books, clothes, and accessories (if you're a reader). Let's investigate why and how to use these things minimally.

Accessories and Apparel

There are three main reasons why wearing clothes, shoes, jewelry, bags, and other accessories in a minimalistic manner is vital. Initially, it saves a significant amount of valuable space in your home and closet that would otherwise be taken up by items you no longer use. It also assists you in discovering your true style and personality. Thirdly, it enables you to live freely and reject other people's opinions of you. You should, therefore, only own well-made, comfortable, and functional clothing items and accessories that truly reflect who you are.

You should put the following advice into practice and discard the following things to determine whether clothing and accessories are just adding to your burden:

Things that have been out of style for longer than a year

Things you don't like

Things you kept because someone said you looked nice in them

Things you believe, as an adult, you should have in your closet

Things you're holding onto merely to add to your collection

Things you want to retain for a special wedding, to use when you are married, or until you lose weight

Things you're holding onto simply in case you misplace a crucial article of apparel

Things you purchased, but you're unsure of how to utilize them and don't want to learn how

Using these methods, you should just throw out anything extra that takes up space in your wardrobe.

Breaking the Cycle of Wants

You must end the cycle of "want." Your personality and image are linked to your clothing, accessories, and makeup choices. You need to improve your appearance, which is the main driver behind your continual purchases of jewelry, shoes, clothes, and similar items. You don't stop the demands and wants that are building inside of you and put them ahead of your true needs because you are worried about what other people think of you, how to impress them, and how to stand out in society. Simply ask yourself what you require. After considering this subject and determining the answer, you should throw away everything more than a desire. Convince yourself that you don't need the frills in life and that getting rid of the extras will bring you one step closer to mental tranquility. You'll be inspired to purge your clothes by this.

Books

If you enjoy reading a lot and are a bookworm, you probably put a lot of effort into creating your library. While this concept is undoubtedly beautiful and regal, hoarding books is the exact reverse of minimalism.

Consider how often you will reread a book once you've finished it. If you answered "many times," then you find that book significant. If the response is "hardly again," it is obvious that you are merely keeping the book to add to your collection rather than using it to learn anything new, benefit from it, or enjoy it repeatedly. What good is it to keep it around when you can't gain anything from anything anymore? Why not give it away and help others benefit from it? In this method, you'll contribute to the upbringing of society and assist others at the same time.

Only the books that have completely changed your old, conservative, and unconstructive mindset and improved you should be kept, along with a few childhood favorites that hold special meaning for you and your family and a few books you wish to give your children to teach them or share a little piece of your childhood with.

Breaking the Cycle of Wants

If you want to read books, it's fantastic. Although you should never part with this priceless gift, you can give up your book-hoarding behavior. Obtain a membership card from a reputable local library and go there often to check out books. When buying new books, only buy what you truly need. For example, you should buy a book if you need it for your research project and can't live without it. Do not add to your collection solely by purchasing new books, though.

The Reasons To Try Minimalism

To Obtain Freedom and Peace of Mind

An extravagant lifestyle is characterized by a fixation on material possessions and an excessive attachment to them. You feel compelled to purchase something every time you see anything exquisite, remarkable, or reasonably priced. In addition, you become anxious about losing something that holds great significance for you. These anxieties and temptations turn you into a mental slave. You let your temptations rule your life rather than living it according to your terms. This frustrates you and causes more tension than you could have imagined.

Adopting a minimalist lifestyle will help you eliminate all the needless tensions and frustrations in your life since you will no longer be attached to worldly belongings and will only keep the items you need. Naturally, you lead a simpler, calmer life that permits you to live freely when you do not feel obligated to give in to your cravings.

To Lead a Meaningful Life

Decluttering your life is necessary for minimalism to separate meaningful items from meaningless ones and dispose of the latter. Your home and life become more organized and simplified when you live with what matters to you. This makes your home a place worth living in by assisting you in creating a more comfortable and welcoming atmosphere.

To Achieve True Happiness

We are diverted from the things our souls genuinely yearn for by the millions of possessions surrounding us. It doesn't take much to make us happy. Instead, we only need to decide to live that way if we want to be content with a small number of things. We are conditioned to always want more because of consumerism and the numerous media biases that permeate our daily lives. We no longer feel content with a few goods, and in an attempt to find happiness, we want more of everything.

The need for more never leads to calm in our lives; it just makes things more stressful because having more means taking care of more things, worrying more about keeping them secure, and even spending more money maintaining them. All of this stresses us out a great deal.

By practicing minimalism, we can free ourselves from the bonds of materialism and provide significance and joy to the things and people who are important to us. Happiness naturally comes from the inside when we focus on what we need rather than what we want.

How to Get Rid of Unwanted Ideas and Thoughts

In addition to clearing your life of unneeded and toxic ideas, opinions, and sentiments that make you long for more and ignore the important things, feelings, and people in your life right now, minimalism also helps you purge your mind of these things. You will never lead a meaningless, extravagant life if you develop a calm attitude that can distinguish between important and meaningless things.

To Concentrate on Appropriate Individuals and Connections

We do not wish to maintain many ties and people, yet we do. We continue to live with them and feel terrible inside because we have hidden agendas or hope to benefit from them. Adopting a minimalist lifestyle can help you escape this suffering.

By practicing minimalism, you may purify and clean up every area of your life, including your relationships. A calm, straightforward, and minimalistic attitude prevents you from pursuing any unethical goals. As a result, you'll let go of everyone taking advantage of you or yourself and devote more of your attention to the connections and people who genuinely bring you joy and love.

Chapter 1: Creating the Attitude

How, then, can you go from being that person who has to have the newest iPhone to understanding that material belongings are not what makes life meaningful? The benefits are clear, but the task at hand is not simple. It will be a refuge in your home. Your family will appreciate the extra time that comes with simplicity, and you will enjoy life more without the pressures. In what way will they benefit? I asked the same thing, so believe me. You've come to the correct spot if your thoughts aren't constantly racing about how you'll pay for Christmas presents for your kids or how you'll pay for life. Your children only have one childhood, and as they become older, they won't remember that one Christmas present that wasn't there. What people want in the here and now are parents who have the time to truly enjoy their children's formative years. Many cannot fulfill this desire because they prefer to provide their children with the financial possessions they feel will improve their lives and work longer hours than they would like to spend with their families.

To truly improve your situation in life, you must first adopt the appropriate mentality. This entails finding a peaceful location and spending 20 minutes there daily, or 15 if possible. I would like you to clear your mind to understand the consequences of depreciation. I want you to sit in a hard chair for twenty minutes daily and focus on breathing. Count to seven as you inhale through your nose, then ten as you exhale. This aids in regulating the quantity of oxygen entering your bloodstream. You likely overoxygenate when you're stressed and unhappy, and this stress will make you more fearful of life. Try to focus solely on your breathing while performing the breathing exercise. Just breathe, ignoring everything else that is happening in the world. If you realize that ideas bother you, acknowledge they are there and learn to disregard them completely. This entails keeping those ideas from running together in your head. Return to focusing on your breathing by pulling yourself back.

There are several advantages to doing this every morning before you go to work. It's worth setting your alarm clock early for, trust me. You are developing the practice of mindfulness, which is being conscious of those few times rather than allowing your thoughts to stray. Even though you might have to coerce yourself into doing this every day, you'll soon notice that a new habit is developing, and you won't even have to think about it—just like when you go to the toilet or perform your ablutions daily. It will just become something you do.

This is significant because it enables you to perceive your life's issues more clearly. You minimize their significance in your life by shutting those cardboard boxes of thinking. This assists you in adopting the proper frame of mind to deal with all of the clutter in your life. You may accomplish more in less time, thanks to your clear thinking.

Why Embrace Minimalism

In this chapter, you will learn the very principles that are the foundation of authentic fulfillment and happiness. The most lovely thing is that you will be free to decide whether the disciplined pursuit of less or the ceaseless chase of material possessions and filling your life with unnecessary objects would bring you true happiness.

Living a Minimalist Lifestyle Increases Your Savings

One major advantage of minimalism, which is the deliberate pursuit of a few things and removing unnecessary extravagance, is that it increases your savings. What does this signify? Almost nothing in our society is free, not even the food or water you eat or the house you live in. Money is necessary for us to pay for products and services, even the ones we have determined are essential, whether we like it or not. This might not be an issue for the wealthy, but for the impoverished or those who barely make ends meet, finding the money to do the things they need to do might be. What if I told you that simplicity allows you to save more money? How? The lesson of minimalism is to eliminate items you don't need or care about and take up valuable space in your life that could be used for other things. It also keeps you from accumulating more of the same items that you have let go of. The savings that come with simplicity extend beyond financial gains. It also saves you a great deal of needless work and emotional investment. You will have fewer things in your life to care for and maintain. Because there are fewer things to take care of, one of the objectives of minimalism is to make cleanup quick and simple.

Aids in Becoming Real

Maybe you're one of those who have so many books in your home that you hardly ever read them or whose contents you can't even begin to understand. One way to deceive yourself could be by collecting works of art that you claim to be knowledgeable about or admire. Alternatively, you can be among those who frequently go to auctions to purchase goods at outrageous costs. Indeed, many individuals share your situation, leading false lives as a status symbol. We would prefer to be called the bookworm who has studied a great deal of classical literature. We want to be known as the woman who owns every designer purse made by a specific Italian company. You might want to be known as the person who owns every fantastic CD released by a certain musician in the 1980s. Most of these folks have one thing in common: they don't truly know anything about the items they collect or how they present themselves. Instead, it results from the admiration they get from those who feed their egos and justify the falsehoods they lead.

Alternatively, it can be because these things offer individuals a sense of importance. In either case, sentimental attachment—rather than true love and interest—is the main reason for maintaining most of these souvenirs.

These people must invest more money, time, and space in the items they gather to maintain the deception. Even when they lack the resources to support or finance such upscale tastes, they are still forced to carry out these actions. Imagine a woman who collects every bag from a specific Italian brand as a pastime. If a new design is out and she doesn't seem to have the money to purchase it, she will use every resource at her disposal to make the purchase—

even if it means her credit card will be destroyed. What is the reason behind her actions? She wants to live up to the delusion she tells herself, even if it means throwing off the harmony of her existence. She appears joyful when her friends are around, but she becomes depressed when they go. She seems to get emotional joy every time she looks at the bags—items that don't increase in value—but in reality, melancholy and financial strain are much more prevalent.

But she can learn how to be content with less by practicing minimalism. When it comes to herself and other people, she can be honest. She is no longer the mastermind behind her downfall. She will learn how to live the truth and cease living a lie via minimalism, enabling her to experience the joy and fulfillment of living the truth.

Chapter: A Guide to Minimalism

When you embrace minimalism, it may be like a refreshing breeze on a hot day that relieves you of the extreme heat you've been feeling and allows you to feel free. Thankfully, and in contrast to what the general public believes, minimalism is not all about being thrifty, giving up anything valuable, and spending the rest of your life eating cheese and bread in a one-room condo. Nope, none of that is what minimalism is. To summarize, minimalism can be described as a tool that helps you fill your life with all the goodness you have been missing.

The core principles of minimalism are being true to and valuing what you want out of life—all the things that make your life easier and more comfortable, all the people you truly love and want in your life, and all the things that truly bring you joy. Another aspect of it is giving up all that does not advance your pleasure, health, peace of mind, personal objectives, or the route that leads to your true wishes.

In a nutshell, minimalism asks you to eliminate everything you don't truly need or want, including all the material belongings, concepts, people, and activities. So, on that, you have been holding onto primarily out of a sense of conceit and the allure of consumerism.

Does that mean that if you detest ice hockey but only play it to appease your boss, you must give it up to be minimalist? Does this imply that you should discard all the pots and pans you have been hoarding but never using? Yes, that does indicate that I see.

The point of minimalism as a style of living is to free yourself from all the ideas, thoughts, beliefs, and superfluous desires that prevent you from moving forward, achieving your goals, being who you truly are, and realizing your true aspirations. For example, even though you may feel delighted when you get an expensive new outfit, you may not want it if you would rather donate the money to your needy buddy. You will discover that you are happier than ever if you begin to listen to your desires.

You can accomplish that by gradually letting go of anything that gives your life no purpose, which is made possible by minimalism. In what ways does minimalism empower you, take away your worries, lessen your stress, and increase your productivity?

You begin to de-clutter your life when you part with items you don't truly need. Your home appears neater and more visually pleasant when there is less clutter in it. This gives your home more room and tranquility while relieving your mind of unneeded worries about organizing, caring for, and safeguarding your belongings. You won't have to worry as much about cleaning and maintaining one fewer couch!

You cease adding needless items to your life when you implement minimalism in various aspects of your existence. This modifies your unwavering views about what it means to live a good life, which supports the development of sound, uplifting beliefs that enable you to create a good life for yourself.

Reducing your social circle to only those you love and respect and honestly care about you is another benefit of minimalism. This guarantees you keep your distance from the doubters and everyone who brings you more damage than good. Your strength, growth mentality, self-worth, and confidence all increase as a result.

Living a minimalist lifestyle also means pursuing your happiness and letting go of all your previous pursuits to pursue unimportant, hidden goals. Social media users are circulating a story that depicts a man at several locations displaying a "Mom, I'm fine" sign. He sold his car, quit his work, and set off to fulfill his lifelong ambition of traveling to other nations. He constantly carried the placard above, which he snapped pictures of to reassure his mother of his safety. While following his interest, he had a terrific time and met many people. Minimalism gave him the freedom to follow his dreams and fulfill his passion.

Give Away, Sell, Donate, And Discard.

What takes place when...
Dealing with whatever you've gathered thus far is the first step towards becoming minimalist. Many items of clothing and kitchenware that we no longer use are just one step away from making our daily lives easier by vanishing.

In other words, we expose ourselves to our emotions at this final time and consider whether it would be better to keep the object. Recall that this value is an exchange value, whereas the use value is the one that interests us. It does not provide us the same benefits as before, so we have reached this stage and are considering taking it away. Time to let it go, I think.

To get things done, there are four simple solutions: sell, give away, donate, and trash away. The good itself, financial demands, available time, and sensitivities all influence our decisions.

Give

Giving is the most selfless course of action by definition. Not only can we donate almost anything, but we are accustomed to providing food and clothing. Consider old phones, office products that can be used for schooling, furniture for underdeveloped nations, and toys for kids. While some groups and non-governmental organizations handle all kinds, others focus on particular resources and have a particular area of activity and goal. Finding the right association might be as easy as asking a well-known organization to recommend other associations that are comparable to yours.

My own experience is giving my library to the prison in Barcelona. The books in the collection included:

Science fiction books.

A good deal of geopolitical reading.

Theoretical articles from the institution.

The prison was a good place to help provide a second opportunity to others who were not as lucky and did not start from the same starting point or chose a different path because it was preserved in perfect shape.

It makes sense that I picked this path over another equally viable one, like sales, as I value and am most sensitive to education. The sale is the default choice for other things. Beyond the personal narrative, it is a reaffirmation that the tendency, stemming from individual inclinations and senses, does not necessarily indicate that one course of action is superior to another.

Clothes donations are more common, as we mentioned. It is feasible to occasionally have a T-shirt or pair of trousers available for donation, even if we don't follow the 'one in, one out' rule and change our clothes less frequently.

It's crucial to resist the need to put off labeled clothing donations and give in to the "I'll do it tomorrow" mentality. Remember that all we need to donate is a shirt or pair of trousers; let's distribute the materials as they become available. Everything adds up. Everything is beneficial.

Giving has a catch associated with it. Purchasing goods for donation is worthless in and of itself because it puts your life or the item's acquisition at a higher value. Although it's one of the finest methods to get rid of stuff, donating isn't a goal in and of itself. So, let's refrain from making purchases to make a later—and possibly even more fictitious—final donation.

Purchase

If we care for our belongings, selling them is the most advantageous action. In the used market, a better-preserving object will command a higher price. Let's now evaluate our turnaround time for sales, among other things.

Selling handbags, coats, televisions, and cell phones makes perfect sense because they are valuable possessions. Even though it works in a batch, it will undoubtedly not compensate for the work, inconvenience, and time required to sell books or t-shirts individually. As previously explained, if we lack sufficient resources, our financial demands will designate this option as the primary one. Likewise, regardless of our circumstances, let's not discount the possibility of a little extra cash from selling these used goods.

If I had mentioned my experience with books and that I would rather donate than have them sold, I would say that I would rather sell technical items like mobile phones, GPS watches, and reflex cameras. I choose their discount over the price range because the things don't directly help underprivileged people. For me, the goal of this deal is a transfer rather than just financial gain. Getting a decent amount for them is not too difficult for me. In this manner, I save time, avoid protracted price talks, and give them a prompt exit without underselling them.

Upgrading to a better model is occasionally the aim of the transaction. If so, we sell before purchasing the new model to avoid shocks. If its sale is delayed, we cannot raise the required funds, or, worse yet, we end up with two items that serve the same purpose.

Chapter 4: Making Daily Life Simpler

The perfect workday routine begins with stretching, getting ready, making the bed, eating breakfast, and formulating a plan. It takes about 1.5 hours to complete. You have to change or omit a step if your morning routine calls for more than that. Things can move more quickly. When it comes to daily life, a minimalist thinks like this.

Developing a Minimalist Mentality

A minimalist believes there should be no more than twenty-four hours daily. Instead, to complete everyday responsibilities within that time, he or she operates quickly, streamlines work, and avoids nonsense.

You wonder if you can make surfaces and rooms cleaner once you declutter. You also consider cutting back on the number of products you use. Continue after those. Consider whether you can streamline, reduce, or expedite your everyday tasks.

For instance, place your cup and plate on the table as you eat. Don't set a coaster and placemat in front of them.

Another illustration would be to leave the alarm clock on the wall or place it atop a dresser. When the alarm goes off, get up and turn it off. Additionally, stretch. If your alarm clock is a fixture on your nightstand, you'll be more likely to hit the snooze button. It can even take a few additional minutes to get out of bed.

Provide concrete answers to the minimalist questions. Then, keep in mind that they are achievable. It's beneficial to minimize the steps or activities and remember what you can and shouldn't do.

Acquiring the Ability to Refuse

Motivational speakers often emphasize embracing every opportunity to avoid missing out on positive experiences. Even if you don't succeed, you will still get some knowledge. If you achieve, you'll feel better about yourself and receive incentives like promotions, pay increases, and recognition. Motivational speakers often overlook that saying no is considerably tougher than saying yes. You only need to glance at the self-assured, aspirational people and the bashful people-pleasers.

Saying yes all the time is not as beneficial as knowing when to accept and when to refuse. People in your vicinity won't mind boundaries if you don't set them. For example, if you work in an office setting but are not a personal secretary, you shouldn't be assigned chores to complete for your boss's personal use. It is not your place to make appointments, send gifts to your superior's family, or even drive them around. If you continue taking on jobs or doing favors, you will be wasting valuable time doing things that could have been more beneficial for you, your office, and yourself.

It makes sense if you find it difficult to say no. Turning down a client, a loved one, or a superior is difficult to consider. You can't help but be concerned that you could let the individual down requesting a favor. Or you worry about the consequences of telling a client or supervisor no. But you should understand that always saying yes can also lead to stress. You are concerned that you took on too much and won't perform well. You will eventually start to worry about the constant demands and wish for them to stop. You'll then question whether they were worth your restless nights.

Don't wait till the circumstance makes you feel angry or indifferent. When you already have a full schedule for the remainder of the day and week, decline tasks. When expressing your reason for refusing, use grace. Although being honest could annoy the other person, everyone should be honest rather than act like everything is alright.

If you cannot attend every family and friend function, don't feel horrible about it. They will understand why you cannot attend some or most events if you are truly important to them. Tell them about your choice as soon as possible to avoid raising expectations. Avoid becoming bogged down in uncertainty, as it will only cause you to think negatively.

You'll deal with less mess if you can also learn to say no to many fads. Steer clear of trendy shoes and clothing that will look out of style in a year or two. Don't base your remodeling on the newest, in-style paint color, furniture style, or décor—all of which will lose their charm with time. As a courtesy, you can make gifts, but let them know they are not required to the next time. You can sell or donate them if they're merely going to be unnecessary clutter in your house. Don't hold onto things merely because they were presents.

It's even more crucial to ignore health-related fads. Most fad diets are unhealthy. If your only goal is to stay in shape, such trendy exercises are neither appropriate nor required. More information about the harmful things you must reject for your health can be found in Chapter 7.

Chapter: Take charge of your time

Work can easily turn into a source of everyday embarrassment. If you've ever experienced frustration in your line of work or your professional endeavors, you will understand exactly where I'm coming from. It can be somewhat taxing to work. Regretfully, many individuals believe that selling your time and labor is the only way to make money.

This is how employment is traditionally defined. When you work for someone else, you are engaging in that. You're trading labor and time for money.

This interpretation of active income reduces you to nothing more than a chicken. Sounds absurd? A chicken won't eat if it doesn't scratch and a worm or grain particle appears. It must, therefore, continually scrape and eat—one scratch, one peck.

It's a subsistence lifestyle. Even if you earn a large salary or more than

$100,000 annually, you still sell your time. See how things turn out after six months of not working. It won't be attractive. Whether you like the reality or not, you sell your labor and time.

There is a substitute.

Active income is an option if you don't want to sell your labor and time. Income can be earned actively on your schedule. Even so, you get to choose your terms for selling your labor and time.

You are not a chicken confined to one spot for eight hours and made to lay what is known as a productivity egg. After completing those eight hours, you exit the coop, eat, watch a little TV, go to bed, and then resume the process day after day, week after week, month after month, and year after year. If you're lucky, the firm may gift you a watch when you retire after 20 years of service. Is it the lofty goal you have set for yourself?

Take solace in knowing you can generate an active income on your terms if that isn't how you envision yourself living. We refer to this as freelancing. You choose your projects, hours, and schedule, but your income stays the same.

You can handle family matters and resume work right before the deadline. You can reschedule the timeframe and discuss it with your client as well. As a freelancer, you have much more freedom in any situation.

You can obtain office work with a results-based timetable to take things further. Put differently, your employer is unconcerned. They don't mind if you leave at 1 pm as long as you deliver the output they paid you for—either eight hours or not.

How Living Minimally Lowers Stress

There is a significant stress reduction when numerous financial obligations are lifted. Stressors related to money, whether one is living alone or with others, are the main cause of anxiety and divorce. Reducing expenses and putting money back in your pocket is quite helpful because finances and money may be stressful.

However, there are other reasons why leading a straightforward, minimalistic lifestyle can help people feel less stressed and anxious.

Visual cues continuously impact our mental states. This explains why "color influence" is a hot psychology issue. Because of things we are taught as youngsters and have imprinted into our fundamental knowledge and neural pathways, colors can elicit particular emotions. Because the associations we developed as children become the basis of so many other, broader forms of information, many individuals identify the color blue with "relief" and red with "anger."

This is also the underlying principle of recognition—the notion that an image might aid in recollecting an experience, a memory, or an emotional reaction. But this function never stops operating. Every time you visually take in something, the things around you elicit an emotional and physical reaction, and having meaningless items in your life might make you feel confined and uncontrollably tight. The visual recall changes from a congested to an open feeling by taking those objects out and making the environment more spacious and open. This can fool the brain into feeling more at ease.

However, leading a minimalist lifestyle implies that you are free from the need to follow fashion trends. By escaping the never-ending cycle of brand-name purchases and upgraded technology, you break free from the constraints of "have to have to be worthy." Who you are is not defined by the things you own. We are all buried with the same thing in the end: ourselves. If your possessions are how you define yourself, you'll constantly feel like you need to spend money. You might not have to feel good enough. This can cause you to feel insecure, careless, and competitive all the time. It can also make you feel anxious all the time.

Furthermore, since you no longer have a way to divert your attention from your difficulties, leading this lifestyle makes you more likely to address the underlying reasons for any troubles you may be experiencing. You can see the real reason for your compulsive shopping—a fear of not being liked and accepted by others—once you stop constantly adding clothing to your expanding closet.

Now that you're not shopping compulsively, you need to deal with the problem head-on to relieve the tension this emotion is bringing you, or at the very least, you can discover trigger scenarios that you can then avoid.

You can finally indulge in activities you genuinely want to, which can relieve stress and help you identify what is important against what is needless. Rather than becoming a slave to material items and the stress they cause, you are free to take care of the things that bring you beauty and to design your life according to your standards and perspective.

The entire voyage also has an amazing component of self-discovery. You can concentrate more on yourself, what you genuinely love, and what you genuinely do not enjoy, even though you may be giving up possessions or bad habits. You can ultimately discover what drives you and manage your life by your internal clock when you look at it without the distracting noise of a cluttered lifestyle or growing financial challenges.

This helps you develop a better sense of self, which can boost confidence and lessen some of people's fears in social situations.

Chapter 3: Getting Started with Minimalism

Decluttering is the first step towards a minimalist lifestyle. Let's examine how you can accomplish that:

Put it in writing.

Write a detailed list of why you want a simpler life. Put your frustration with debt collectors in writing. Do you find it bothersome that you don't get to spend much time with your children? Don't forget to write this down. Are you frequently too anxious and tense to get a good night's sleep? Additionally, put it in writing. These are your "whys," which will give you the willpower to endure difficult times.

Establish a clutter-free area.

This one functions wonderfully. The spot could be your nightstand, the kitchen table, a countertop, or just one drawer. Take inspiration from this area to reduce and simplify your life. Extend this zone daily, just a bit, as your fondness for that pure, clear surroundings grows. This method transforms a clutter-free kitchen drawer into a clutter-free kitchen area, which becomes a clutter-free household.

Bring three large grocery store boxes home.

Mark one box as "keep," another as "sell," and a third as "charity." Additionally, you should get a sizable trash can, ideally lined, into which you will place all items that are either too worn out to be used anymore or broken and cannot be utilized. Making the house more spacious is the real objective.

Establish a time limit for the meeting.

The recommended duration is 15 to 60 minutes. Set a timer and ensure you don't start more work than you can finish in the allotted time. Stop when the timer goes off, tidy up, and then take a short break—say, fifteen minutes. It's imperative to take a break to avoid burnout. After your break, you might always choose to give it another shot or not.

Less Is More: Chapter 2 - Teaching Your Children

Have you ever been behind a child who couldn't stop asking questions in the store? Are you one of those people who, while whimpering and pleading for something, has to touch everything on every shelf? Alternatively, perhaps you have endured a child who is always yelling and a desperate parent doing all in their power to get their child to stop, including offering them candy or toys.

Perhaps you were that desperate and frustrated parent. Perhaps you felt awkward and unsure of what to do. A minimalist lifestyle might be beneficial. It won't address every issue you're having as a parent. It's not a foolproof remedy. But knowing how to handle those in-store meltdowns can be helpful. This might even prevent you from ever becoming a new parent.

For Recently Married Couples

Even before we look into those stunning eyes, our first instinct as parents is to give them everything they could need or desire. We want to be ready for every eventuality that may arise. Thus, we make purchases. We purchase items like cribs and car seats that we are certain we will require.

We purchase necessities like toys and storage containers just because they're adorable. We keep going overboard as they get older. When babies sit up, we are happy and buy them chairs, bouncers, and walkers. Before long, it appears that you have several babies while, in fact, you just have one.

This marks the start. They soon have so many toys that they never even play with them. They own drawers filled with clothing that they outgrow after wearing it once. We have already introduced them to an extravagant world.

As they grow into toddlers, we misinterpret their signs. Even when we know they are exhausted and have errands to run, we push them. Next, you find yourself in the store with a highly demanding toddler, giving him toys, candies, or anything else that would buy you a little extra time to get what you need. We've educated children that material possessions equate to happiness.

They take advantage of it when they are mature enough to understand that. Preventing it entirely is the simplest method to ensure that it never occurs. Make a simple daily schedule. They are important. Remind them of their importance by not pressuring them. While there might occasionally be some inconvenience, it is worth it.

BEING FREE FROM MODERN MANIA IS MINIMALISM.

The pace of our world is quite fast. We are overly anxious, harried, and hurried.

We put in a lot of overtime and work hard to pay the bills, yet our debt only grows. We multitask while rushing from one duty to the next, but we never finish everything. We are constantly in contact with others through our cell phones, but genuine, life-altering relationships are still elusive.

Living a minimalist lifestyle releases us from the contemporary frenzy to live life at a faster pace. It is liberated to step back. It aims to preserve only the necessities. It aims to preserve the important and eliminate the frivolous. And in doing so, it elevates the deliberate pursuits that enrich life.

DUPLICITY-FREEDOM IS MINIMALISM.

Most individuals live in deception, even if it's not something they consciously select. They lead three different lives: one focused on their family, another on their coworkers, and still another on their neighbors. Depending on their circumstances, their chosen lifestyle needs them to project a particular outward image. The latest marketing initiative or their employer's expectations toss them around.

A basic life, on the other hand, is cohesive and reliable. It has acquired a way of life that is entirely adaptable to any circumstance. Friday nightlife is the same as Sunday morning life, and it is the same as Monday morning life. It is steady, steady, and unwavering. It functions in every situation.

Substance Minimalism Is International.

Celebrities are idolized in our world. They are filmed for television, interviewed on the radio, and shot for magazines. Many people are envious of them and view their lives as the ideal. The media does not support people who lead minimalist lives in the same manner. They are incompatible with the consumerist culture that politicians and businesses support. They yet lead a desirable and welcoming life.

Most people are focused on achieving success, glitz, and celebrity, while minimalism speaks to us in a quieter, more subdued way. It challenges us to enjoy life more, slow down, and consume less. Furthermore, we frequently realize that we have been pursuing the wrong goals our entire lives when we see someone with a simpler lifestyle.

Organising Techniques of a Minimalist

Most people view modern life as a challenging journey through which we must persevere, but what if I told you that it doesn't have to be? You can develop an appreciation for life's little pleasures.

These are the five talents you may learn to live a simpler, more satisfying life for yourself. These are general applications that apply to everyone and are not complicated at all:

1-Awareness

Most of the time, people are unaware of how they spend their time and how they become disconnected from the present. People jump from one scenario to the next without stopping to think about what might be the greater picture. When faced with a crisis, we are sometimes too preoccupied with getting things done to stop and think about why we are doing things.

Do you need this many items? Do you want to spend your time this way? These are questions you should ask yourself.

Utilize these questions to help you develop a vision for your life, and reflect on it before you begin your day to determine the ideal method to begin that will further your personal growth.

Having a system with everything you need to serve as a guide is crucial.

2. Pay Attention

Individuals must begin choosing wisely how to spend their time. However, even those who have made these wise decisions occasionally become disoriented during the day. Throughout the day, various obstacles could come up; if you're not alert, you might not see them coming and won't be able to escape them.

3-Restrictions

You can set boundaries for yourself by two methods: (1) by limiting the number of tasks on your list that you must do. (2) Setting a weekly time limit on how much time you should dedicate to work. To make the most of your free time, I advise limiting how much you work and using it for other activities.

4-Set priorities.

When someone lists everything they need to get done, most things are not as critical as they first seem. You can enumerate ten or twenty distinct things to perform. Identifying which jobs are more urgent than the others will help you focus on completing the most important ones instead of trying to do everything at once.

5-Bargaining

Expectations play a role in negotiations, and occasionally, your expectations may greatly impact your capacity to simplify your day. Sometimes, you could expect to complete all of these things during the day, but you have to compromise on what can be done now and what can wait until another day.

You have to bargain for two things while negotiating: (1) your expectations, which is to expect to do the most critical tasks first, and (2) your expectations with everyone else, which is to enlist the help of individuals in your immediate vicinity.

Chapter 3: A Simple Morning Routine that Fits into an 80/20 The Pareto Law

The morning ritual or routine is crucial for productivity and overcoming the day. The way you begin your day matters a lot. Things won't go well the remainder of the day if you start the day off badly. I place great importance on morning routines and rituals. It assists me in placing the remainder of the day in the proper context.

Pareto's Law: 80/20 Regulate

Tim Ferriss introduced me to this concept, which states that 20% of actions produce 80% of the intended outcomes. An Italian economist, Vilfredo Pareto, is credited with creating Pareto's Law. You may use this idea in every aspect of your life. If we write down every job in our daily routine and concentrate only on 20% of the most critical ones, we will accomplish 80% of our goals in the morning ritual and routine. Being effective is more important than being efficient, which is acting morally rather than acting morally in every situation. By doing this, we simplify our routines and duties to the key elements that will enable us to achieve success on a large scale.

Logistics and consistency are the easiest things for me to control. That is to say, I have to set myself up to complete my morning ritual and habit with minimal effort. Having stuff close by makes everything accessible and achievable. And all the everyday rituals and habits that need to be followed consistently.

Consistently carrying out our morning rituals or routines will help us establish them as habits and improve our chances of success over time.

Routine That's Motivational & Positive

It's imperative to start the morning on a high note because it will determine the whole quality of the day, whether good or terrible. Although it may require much willpower to complete tasks daily, a solid morning routine makes it much simpler to do tasks organically when you start the day in a happy, upbeat, and motivated state of mind. It won't require much work to guide it throughout the day.

Each individual is unique. People simply have different wiring. Some people prefer the morning, while others prefer the evening. For me, the morning is when I'm most productive. I just want to relax and unwind after eating a hearty dinner at night. Most likely, finish a glass of red wine and end the day.

Additionally, I am aware of some folks who work better at night. You only need a deep self-awareness to determine what is effective for you and what is not. The secret is to keep trying.

Chapter 2: Getting Ready for the Shift

Depending on your inclination towards hoarding or accumulating things, you may find this transition difficult. As a result, it's critical that you emotionally and even physically ready yourself for the significant shift that is about to occur before you begin. In light of this, let's examine how to physically acquire the tools you'll need to break free from your hoarding behaviors and emotionally become ready to do so.

Mental Readiness

You have already made a significant step towards a clear, clutter-free future by getting this book and following its advice. However, this does not always mean you are prepared to make sacrifices to overcome this unpleasant tendency. As such, give yourself some mental time to become ready. You should have determined what you think could be the root of this illness by now.

As discussed in Chapter One, you might be experiencing feelings of inadequacy or loneliness. Ask them to help you identify the issue if you cannot locate its source.

After that, mentally inventory the things you have hoarded and consider why you have them and how they fit into your life. Most of the things you've retained throughout the years will likely serve no functional purpose, and you won't feel particularly attached to them emotionally. You'll probably discover things you had entirely forgotten about that only really had sentimental worth when you decided to preserve them when you began going through the tangible stuff. It should be simpler to let go of the things you have been holding onto once you realize they are worthless.

When your mind begins to justify why something is valuable, push yourself to critically examine the accuracy of those assertions. Is it really that significant what you wore—torn and torn—when you were a virgin years ago? Or is it something that can be harmful to your health in addition to taking up cabinet space? This also applies to the stack of newspapers arranged on your couch. Sometimes, when you enjoy each other's company, a genuine, live person may sit there instead of dwelling on the past. You must accept that you will get rid of most of your belongings. We will go into more detail about certain objects in the upcoming chapter, but for now, you just need to accept that you are holding onto things pointlessly.

This is the step that might cause the greatest anxiety, so it would be a good idea to drink herbal teas or look for other ways to help you de-stress and concentrate on the task at hand.

Chapter 2: Advantages of a Minimalist Way of Life

Now that we have a rudimentary understanding of minimalism's psychology let's talk about its benefits and maybe pique your interest.

tranquility of mind

First of all, minimalism's positivity on an emotional and mental level is one of its main advantages. Eliminating unneeded items and people from our lives also helps us eliminate the anxious thoughts associated with them. As a result, it calms your nerves and enables you to start realizing what is important. Greater peace of mind follows from your natural tendency to become calmer when you give up on wanting more and remove things that bring negativity.

Furthermore, as numerous studies have demonstrated, eliminating negative thoughts makes more significant mental space available for nurturing positive, healthy thoughts that enhance your psychological, emotional, and physical well-being.

Author Charles Spurgeon (1834) said, "You say, 'If I had a little more, I should be very satisfied.'" This is a true statement. You commit an error. You wouldn't be happy if your possessions were multiplied if you weren't happy with what you had. If we can't be happy with what we already have, how can we be satisfied with more?

Budgetary Control

Living a financially calm existence is challenging due to stagnating wages, increased unemployment, and ever-increasing expenses. Furthermore, your unquenchable needs can drive you to borrow money to support your lifestyle if you spend more than you make. All these things might make life difficult as you feel like you have to keep up with everyone, yet your finances don't allow you to follow the crowd.

But when you adopt a minimalist lifestyle, these impacts improve since they help you reassess your requirements, wants, and purchases by limiting your possessions to what is necessary. It becomes easier to live within your means without feeling pressured to keep up with the "Joneses" when your expectations and wants diminish and your spending drops. This, in turn, makes it simpler to make wise financial decisions and lead a financially responsible and contented life.

Chapter 4
"Know Thyself" – Ancient Greece

Identify & explore: What are we identifying and exploring? We are identifying the core values and beliefs we want to govern the sector of our lives in question. We also want to explore which values are currently driving our behaviors. The reason for the study of these intangibles is that beliefs create values, and values create behaviors. Behaviors not created from values or values not created from beliefs do not last. So, if we build off of a good foundation, our changes will last. Knowing which of our values to regard as a core value is the first step to embarking on the Minimalist Lifestyle. Sometimes, finding our core values is as easy as assigning them. However, there are situations where identifying our values may not be as straightforward. Sometimes, we may feel a stranger to ourselves, unable to account for why we do what we do. How do we identify our values when we don't understand ourselves? One tip I could offer is to play a game called "Why Does This Matter?"

To play, you take the components of a sector of your life, whether tangible or intangible and ask, "Why does this matter?" Then you take the answer and say, "Why does this matter?" Then, you repeat the question as many times as it takes to get to the root of why this is in your life. Then, you can ascertain if what you discover is something you want to make a core value or not. This game can be very useful to investigate which thoughts and beliefs influence your clutter.

I am a big proponent of choosing which values you want to become core. Approaching my life with a high level of intentionality has proven more rewarding. However, you must choose from current values and play within you if you want lasting change. Beliefs create values, and values create behaviors. You can't just make this stuff up.

So, how do we choose which values to regard as "core?" This question is incredibly personal, but I will offer my perspective. As you inventory your behaviors, time spent, and "stuff," you can discover much about your beliefs. I find it interesting that some of these behaviors are often sound and true, but the opposite could be said at times. I have found beliefs and values founded on hurt, bad experiences, and even lies. When ascertaining which values to assign as core, I would recommend choosing values that are:

True

Acknowledging the best in you

Acknowledging the best in others

I recommend reducing the core values for any sector of your life to 3 or 4. These don't have to be perfect initially, as you will see later in this book. What is important is that you try and test. Over time, you will be able to see if the core values chosen allow you to build a lifestyle that is "you." For clarity, I will apply this step to the story of the first business I bought.

Minimise: Decluttering And Reducing.

After the first chapter, you should be able to identify the true situation of your non-physical and tangible belongings and your objective. We want to decide what is vital and what is not as we begin minimizing and tidying up. You can still follow the minimalist approach and find inspiration even if unsure about your objective.

These are fundamental ideas about keeping things neat and organized, as these are the cornerstones of minimalism. Perhaps you are one of those people who finds it difficult to distance themselves from objects, or you find it difficult to return items to their original positions after using them; perhaps you procrastinate endlessly, wanting to realize an excessive number of ideas, feeling overwhelmed and unable to complete tasks; perhaps you are simply tired and uninspired, hiding in a self-made mess (a fitting Japanese proverb: The mess in your room corresponds to the mess in your heart). Within the minimalist lifestyle, disorder is unimaginable and must be ruthlessly destroyed both internally and outside.

Life involves tidying up, which is made easier by structure and order. You have the chance to create space so that new things can happen. In what other way might you obstruct everything with burdens from the past? In minimalism, "new things" are not limited to material possessions; they can also refer to new interests, an exciting trip, a new friendship, etc. Learning how to establish a structured order without reverting to negligence is possible after a few days or weeks. It is possible for anyone. Minimalism makes This lesson easier because there are fewer possessions to keep oneself busy. In this light, minimalism is ideal for people who are too lazy to tidy up. By adhering to a few basic principles, everyone can live in order and feel free, thanks to minimalism.

Let's start by examining the typical mess at home or the workplace. Either a behavioral issue (the jacket needs to be hung up, not flung over the sofa) or an attitude issue (tidying up is vital, and I want to order) is present in the person who is always cleaning up. When a system is in place, it only takes one cleaning to get used to the new, fundamental order and to clean up correctly once; after that, there is no need to clean up again (more on that later).

Chapter 3: Why Do I Need to Clear Out?

I can't think of a good reason not to declutter, even though there are many excellent ones. Living a chaotic life can result in major health issues like melancholy, anxiety, and heart disease while living a clutter-free life can make you happier, healthier, and more focused, according to scientific research. Why would you not want to simplify your life and reduce noise?

Organising can

Boost your sense of self-worth.

The fact that decluttering might be daunting is one of the reasons you might find it challenging. You could feel overwhelmed when you take in your whole home and wonder if decluttering is feasible. When you declutter properly, removing stuff can make you feel like you've accomplished something and give you the extra confidence to take on the remainder of the house. Decluttering as you go or room by room is a common suggestion. Allow the breeze of decluttering to carry you. Individual processes differ, but once you figure out a method that works for you, you'll move through your house easily. It won't always be simple to let go; occasionally, we may become sentimental and connected to insignificant objects that aren't necessary. You can keep them if they hold significance for you (remember, we're attempting to be minimalists here). Often, muster the courage to treasure, express gratitude for, and part with these belongings. Letting go is a sign of strength, giving you the courage to move forward.

Boost communication in partnerships.

You wouldn't think that having clutter would have that much of an impact on your life, much less the lives of those around you. Yes, that is accurate. How can you expect to take care of yourself and your relationships with others if you aren't even caring for your own space? You need to be free to live as you see fit to be a good friend, partner, or parent. You run the risk of classifying the people in your life as things that clutter your life and give you distress if you are unsure about this.

In another way, it can be challenging for you and others to be expressive when you create a noisy and distracting environment. Let's take the example of a married person. You have full-time jobs and are frequently worn out when you get home. You drudge into the kitchen to prepare dinner, consisting of a pot of noodles and premade pasta sauce. You check your phone while hunching over the kitchen chair, lazily reading through other people's lives. Your partner is performing the same thing while seated across from you. This is your life in a disorganized setting. Imagine it now clear of clutter:

www.ingramcontent.com/pod-product-compliance
Lightning Source LLC
Chambersburg PA
CBHW052144110526
44591CB00012B/1846